Whale Strandings
A Mystery of Nature

Contents

Written by Claire I

Collin

GW00578052

1 The story of a stranding

VOLUNTEERS HELP IN WHALE RESCUE

Volunteers in Sri Lanka worked through the night to save 100 pilot whales that became stranded in shallow water. The whales were spotted in the afternoon. "They looked like a dark patch on the **horizon**," said a fisherman. "Then they moved towards the shore. We tried to push them back, but they kept returning."

Whale strandings are regularly in the news. This one had a happy ending, and all but four of the whales were saved. But what are whale strandings and why do they happen?

Did you know?
Around 2,000 whales **get stranded** every year.

2 What is a stranding?

Whale strandings happen in different ways. Sometimes a **beached** whale is discovered dead on the shore. Usually it died at sea, either from sickness or injury, and its body washed up onto the beach. This is one kind of stranding.

a beached North Pacific right whale: the powerful sea creature now lies on the Northern Californian shore

Whales also get stranded in cold oceans when the surface of the water freezes above them. Why would this be dangerous for whales?

But live, healthy whales get stranded too. They seem to deliberately swim in to the shore and then get stuck in shallow water. Sometimes, it's just one or two whales, but sometimes it's a large group: this is called a mass stranding.

3 Why is stranding dangerous?

Whales are mammals and breathe in air, so why are they at such risk when they get stranded?

The greatest danger is their size. Whales live in the sea, where the saltwater supports their massive weight.

beluga whale

Did you know?

Well-fed, healthy whales are much more likely to survive a stranding.

When a whale is out of water, its weight starts to crush its lungs and other important **organs**.

This beached Southern right whale needs to be refloated as soon as possible.

Another danger comes from their blubber – a thick layer of fat under their skin. It quickly causes beached whales to overheat. Whales need to stay cool and moist. Can you think how rescuers could help them?

bottlenose whale

7

4 Where do strandings happen?

Beached whales are found all over the world but most mass strandings seem to happen along the coasts of Australia, New Zealand, Chile and the east coast of North America, as shown in the yellow shading on the map. They sometimes happen in northern Europe, too.

ARCTIC OCEAN

North Sea

NORTH AMERICA

EUROPE

A

ATLANTIC OCEAN

AFRICA

PACIFIC OCEAN

SOUTH AMERICA

IND

ATLANTIC OCEAN

CHILE

SOUTHERN OCEAN

Whales are magnificent creatures, and some species are falling in number, so it's upsetting when they get stranded. Why do they do this? We'll try to answer that question, but first we need to know more about whales and their undersea world.

Whale strandings are nothing new. This painting from 1617 shows a stranded whale on a beach in the Netherlands.

PACIFIC OCEAN

AUSTRALIA   OCEANIA

Tasmania

NEW ZEALAND

Did you know?

In 2021, a whale got stranded in London. It had swum up the river Thames.

5 The whale family

Whales are a group of marine mammals. There are over 90 different species in all, including dolphins and porpoises. Like all mammals, whales have lungs and need to breathe in air. They swim up to the surface to breathe before diving down again.

Whales come in different sizes: the blue whale is the biggest animal ever to have lived on Earth.

bottlenose dolphin – 2–4 metres

orca – 8 metres

humpback whale – 16 metres

blue whale – 30 metres

A whale breathes through a blowhole on the top of its head.

blowhole

Did you know?

The bottlenose whale can make one breath last for up to two hours.

6 A life in the sea

Whales can be found in all the world's oceans, from the warm tropics to the icy poles. Their bodies help them to survive in water. They all have a long, smooth body with a large paddle-like tail. They all have a blowhole on the top of their head and a thick layer of fat called blubber under their skin. Can you think how these features have helped whales to live in the sea?

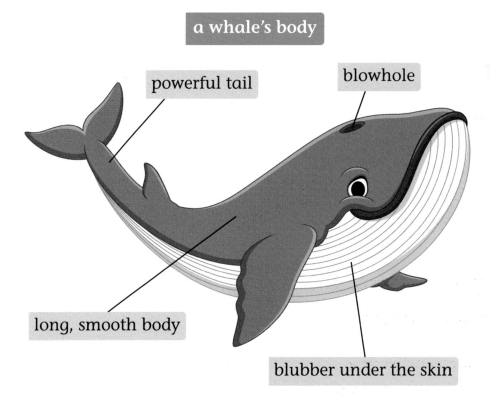

a whale's body

powerful tail

blowhole

long, smooth body

blubber under the skin

A minke whale powers through the water.

Did you know?

A whale's tail is called a fluke.

13

Solitary or sociable?

Different whales have different lifestyles. Some whales, like humpback and blue whales, prefer to live alone and only come together to **breed**. These **solitary** whales are less likely to get stranded.

Blue whales usually live alone.

Other whales, such as dolphins, orcas and sperm whales, live in close-knit groups called pods. The pod members follow a leader and often play and hunt together. These **sociable** whales are more likely to get stranded. Can you think why?

a pod of female sperm whales with their calves

Did you know?

There are about 15–20 sperm whales in a pod.

Sight or sound?

It's hard to see in deep water because it's very dark. As a result, whales rely more on their hearing. Sound travels well through water and is much more important to whales than sight.

A humpback whale's song can be heard hundreds of kilometres away.

Whales are big-brained animals and like to **communicate** with one another. They use sound to do this. Orcas whistle to other members of their pod. Solitary whales communicate, too. They make long, deep calls, known as whale songs, to try and attract a distant mate.

Did you know?
Orcas recognise each other by their whistle, just as we recognise people by their voice.

A world of sound

Sound helps whales to sense the world around them. They have a special skill called echolocation.

How does echolocation work?

1 A whale makes a clicking noise. This sends out **sound waves** through the sea.

2 When the sound waves hit an object – perhaps a rock, a squid or a ship – echoes bounce back to the whale.

3 The whale's brain uses these echoes to build a picture of its surroundings. It "sees" where objects are.

Echolocation is vital for whales, but what would happen if it went wrong? How might it cause a stranding?

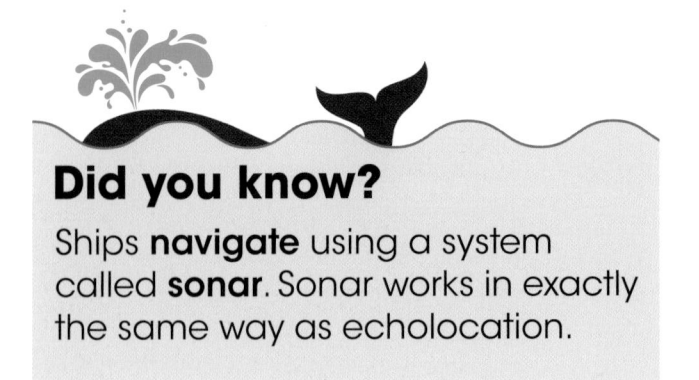

Did you know?

Ships **navigate** using a system called **sonar**. Sonar works in exactly the same way as echolocation.

Key

sound waves from whale

echoes

World travellers

Whales are long-distance travellers. Many of them journey every year between colder and warmer waters. Why do they do this?

Cold seas are rich in food so whales feed and grow well there. Warmer seas are easier places to breed and raise a calf. Travelling to feed and breed is called migration.

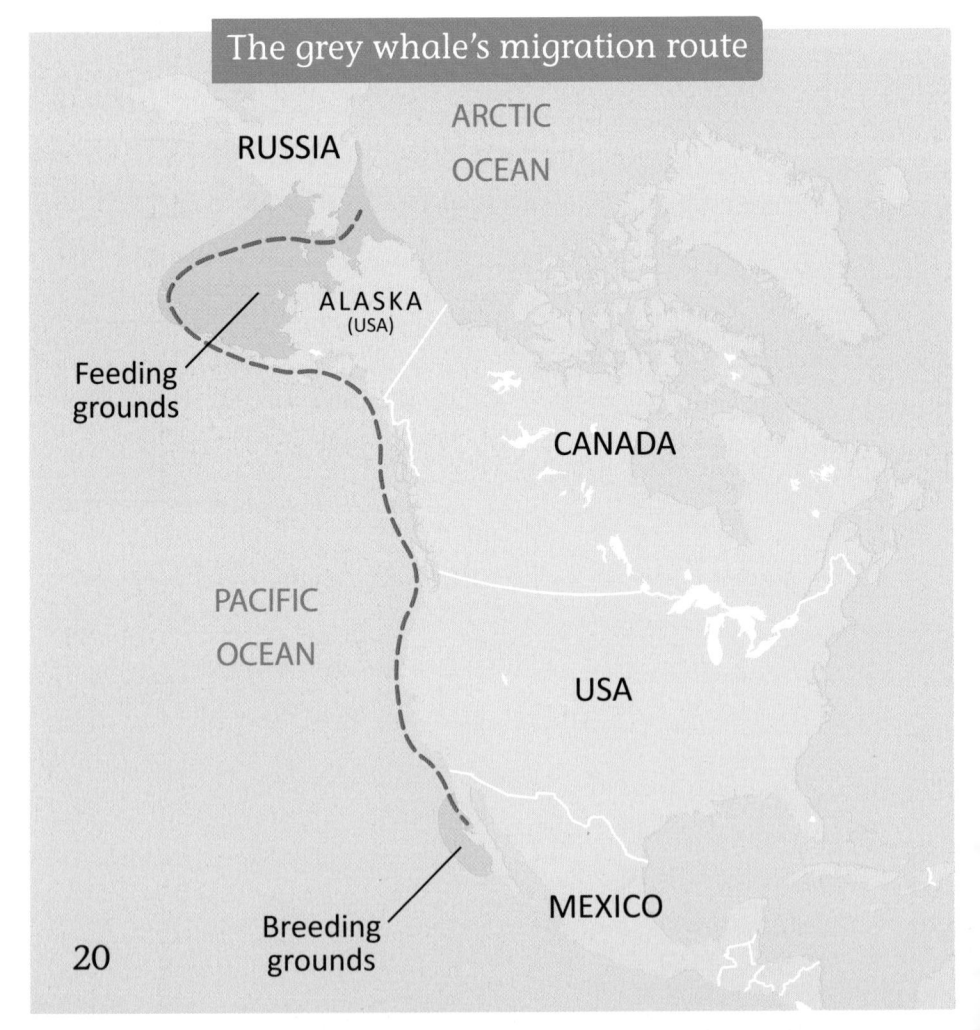

The grey whale's migration route

ARCTIC OCEAN

RUSSIA

ALASKA (USA)

Feeding grounds

CANADA

PACIFIC OCEAN

USA

Breeding grounds

MEXICO

Migration story

Grey whales spend the winter in the warm seas of Mexico. They breed and have their young here.

In early summer, the whales migrate north to the **Arctic**, where the seas are full of food.

Did you know?

Grey whales' return journey is around 16,000 kilometres long.

How do whales navigate?

It's easy to get lost when you're on a journey. So how do whales navigate as they travel through the ocean?

A compass arrow points north.

People use a compass to navigate. A compass arrow swings north because metals deep inside Earth make the planet work like a magnet. Scientists suspect that whales have some kind of compass inside them, which gives them a good sense of direction. But could it sometimes go wrong?

Earthquakes and changes in the Sun can make compasses fail.

But would this cause whales to get stranded?

What do you think?

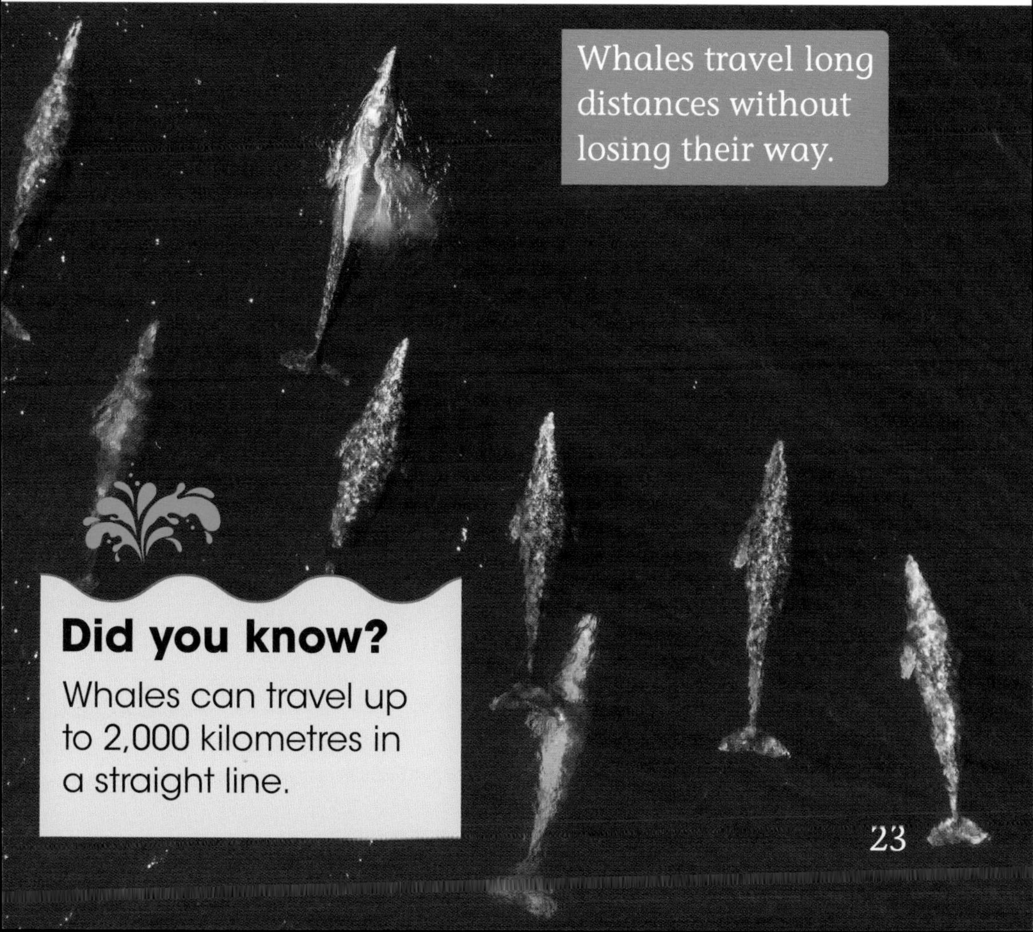

Whales travel long distances without losing their way.

Did you know?

Whales can travel up to 2,000 kilometres in a straight line.

7 Pilot whales: a stranding

Now we know more about whales, let's look at another stranding story. Can you make sense of what's going on?

In September 2020, about 500 pilot whales were stranded on sandbanks off Tasmania. People quickly came to their rescue. As the tide came in, they put slings under the whales and pulled them off the sand. The size of the animals and bad weather made the rescue difficult, but by the end of five days, 108 whales had been saved.

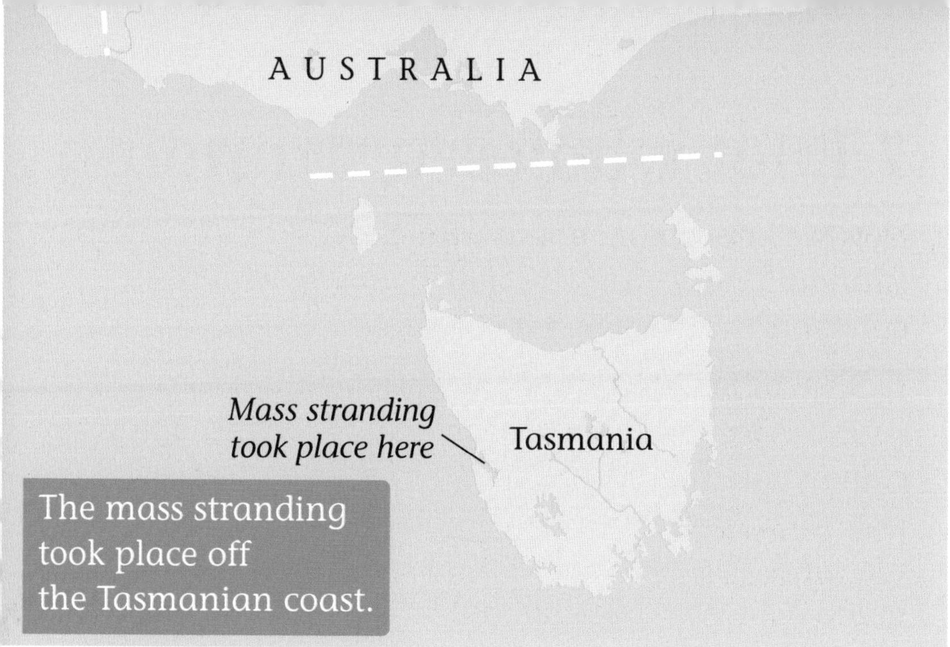

AUSTRALIA

*Mass stranding
took place here* \ Tasmania

The mass stranding
took place off
the Tasmanian coast.

Did you know?

Pilot whales are up to six metres long
and weigh
the same as
two cars.

25

Pilot whales: why did they strand?

Scientists have come up with some possible answers for the mass stranding:

- Pilot whales live in large pods and like to stick together. If the pod leader swims into shallow water, the other whales are likely to follow. But why would the leader make this mistake?

Did you know?

There are up to 1,000 pilot whales in a pod.

- Maybe the leader was sick. **Parasites** can infect a whale's brains and ears. This could affect the leader's judgement or hearing.

- Echolocation might be to blame. Echoes don't bounce clearly off shallow bays and sandbanks. Maybe this misled the leader?

A sick leader can put an entire pod in danger.

Did you know?
The stranding in 2020 was the largest in Australia's history.

8 How to rescue stranded whales

Step 1: Pour water over the whales to keep them cool and moist.

Step 2: Dig **trenches** to help the whales lie upright rather than on their side.

Step 3: As the tide comes in, put large slings under the whales.

Step 4: When the water is knee-deep, drag the whales off the sand.

Step 5: When the water is waist-deep, rock the whales from side to side.

Step 6: Release all the animals together.

Step 7: Link arms and make a human chain to prevent the whales returning.

Rescuers slap the water noisily after they have released whales. Can you think why?

9 Dolphins: a stranding

Dolphins are often found in the seas off England's southwest coast. In June 2008, a large number of dolphins suddenly swam into a large **harbour**, clicking and squealing in panic. They swam round and round in circles before heading up small rivers. Many soon got stranded on the banks.

Rescuers refloated most of the dolphins but, sadly, 26 did not survive. They were healthy animals with no sign of injury. What made them swim into the harbour? Why did they leave their ocean home?

Falmouth °

Falmouth Bay

Key

Dolphin sightings

Dolphins: why did they strand?

Scientists investigated the stranding. They know that small whales often swim to the shore when they are being chased by sharks, but no sharks were seen that day. However, 20 warships, a submarine and army helicopters were out at sea, taking part in a training exercise. How do you think this could have affected the dolphins, given what you know?

warships on a training drill

Did you know?
Ships use sonar to find enemy submarines.

Ships use powerful sonar to explore the ocean.
Perhaps the sound waves confused the dolphins?

The warships may have fired **torpedoes**.
Could an explosion have frightened the dolphins
and triggered the stranding?

Low-flying helicopters
are very noisy.

10 Does noise disturb whales?

Scientists have investigated how whales react to human noise. The scientists played loud sounds in places where whales were resting or feeding. The whales immediately stopped what they were doing, rushed to the surface and swam away. What do you gather from that?

The seas have become noisy places. Thousands of ships criss-cross the oceans, using sonar to navigate. There is drilling on the seabed for wind farms and pipelines. Drilling for oil creates a lot of noise under the water. If whales are disturbed by noise, perhaps they panic, mistake where they are and end up getting stranded? What do you think?

Whales are disturbed by the drilling and traffic around oilrigs.

Did you know?

Whales can suffer hearing loss if they swim to the surface too quickly.

11 Grey whales: a stranding

In October 1988, a hunter in Alaska found three grey whales trapped by ice in the Arctic Ocean. The whales were desperately swimming to the surface to keep open a breathing hole. Why? What did they need in order to survive?

Whales stranded here

Utqiagvik (Barrow)

ALASKA
(USA)

Anchorage

Local people came to the rescue. They cut a pathway of air holes and tried to lure the whales out to sea. But the whales didn't move. Eventually, an icebreaker ship smashed a channel through the ice. By then, one of the whales had died, but the other two were soon seen swimming towards the open sea.

Did you know?

Whales can survive in seas that are two degrees Celsius below freezing point.

Locals cut breathing holes in the ice.

One of the trapped whales surfaces for air.

Grey whales: why did they strand?

Every year, thousands of grey whales migrate to and from the Arctic. Why did these three get stranded? Let's look at some of the suggestions.

The whales were young; one of them was less than a year old. Perhaps, as they searched for food, they wandered too far from the other, older whales. Then, when the temperature dropped very suddenly, they were too young to sense the water freezing. Or maybe they just preferred to keep feeding rather than migrate. What do you think?

Older whales sense when it's time to migrate. The water grows colder and the animals they feed on begin to disappear.

Did you know?

Grey whales eat very little for five months after they leave the Arctic. They use all their energy to migrate and bring up a calf instead.

12 Natural causes of strandings

So why do whale strandings happen? There are often natural causes.

- Whales may get stranded because of old age, sickness or injury, or simply because they mistake where they are.

- A pod of whales may follow its leader or respond to a sick whale's call.

- Whales sometimes get stranded after chasing fish or seals into shallow waters.

- Stormy seas can drive whales into the shore and up on the beach.

- Smaller whales can swim to the shore to escape from sharks.

- Echolocation may mislead whales. It's less reliable in shallow, sandy bays.

- Perhaps earthquakes or changes on the Sun upset the whale's inner compass and lead them astray.

13 Human causes, human help?

But not all strandings have natural causes. Sonar, drilling and explosions disturb and even panic whales so they end up getting stranded. How can we avoid this?

New laws could ban ships from places where whales are known to gather. Workers drilling on the seabed could build up noise gradually, giving whales the chance to move away.

To many people, whales are special. These intelligent, sociable animals communicate and bond with one another, and take great care of their young. By reducing whale strandings, we will help to protect these magnificent creatures.

Glossary

Arctic the land and sea around the North Pole

beached washed up onto a beach, either dead or alive

breed to produce young

communicate to share information with others

earthquakes shakings of the ground caused by movements inside Earth

harbour a protected part of the sea near the coast, where boats can be left

get stranded when whales are beached, or get stuck under ice or trapped in shallow water

horizon where the land meets the sky

navigate to find how to get somewhere

organs parts of the body with a special purpose

parasites tiny animals that live and feed on another animal

sociable enjoying being with others

solitary spending a lot of time alone

sonar equipment on a ship that uses sound waves to work out where things are in the sea

sound waves waves of sound that travel through air, water or solids

torpedoes cylinder-shaped weapons/missiles fired from an underwater vessel

trenches long, narrow ditches

Index

Why do you think whales get stranded?

NORTH
AMERICA

SOUTH
AMERICA

PE

ASIA

AFRICA

OCEANIA

Ideas for reading

Written by Christine Whitney
Primary Literacy Consultant

Reading objectives:
- be introduced to non-fiction books that are structured in different ways
- listen to, discuss and express views about non-fiction
- retrieve and record information from non-fiction
- discuss and clarify the meanings of words

Spoken language objectives:
- participate in discussion
- speculate, hypothesise, imagine and explore ideas through talk
- ask relevant questions

Curriculum links: Science: Animals; Writing: Write for different purposes

Word count: 2564

Interest words: stranded, beached

Resources: paper and pencils

Build a context for reading

- Ask the group if anyone has ever seen a whale in real life. Has anyone seen a whale on TV or in a film? Ask them to work in pairs and list five facts about whales.
- Ask for a volunteer to explain the meaning of the word *stranded* or *strandings*. Can a member of the group use the word correctly in a sentence?
- Encourage children to look closely at the front cover of the book. What do they think is happening?
- Read the blurb on the back cover. Ask the group to suggest why it is that whales get themselves stranded.

Understand and apply reading strategies

- Turn to the contents page and read through the different chapters in the book. Ask for volunteers to say which Chapter they are most interested in reading and why.
- Read together up to the end of Chapter 3. Challenge children to explain why whales get stranded and why it is dangerous for the whales when this happens.